MR BENN'S
Little Book of Life

D1081209

MR BENN'S
Little Book of Life

Tess Read

ARROW

Published by Arrow Books in 2001

1 3 5 7 9 10 8 6 4 2

Copyright © Text Tess Read 2001

Copyright © Illustrations David McKee 2001

Tess Read has asserted her right under the Copyright, Designs and
Patents Act, 1988 to be identified as the author of this work

First published in the United Kingdom by
Arrow Books in 2001

Arrow Books
The Random House Group Limited
20 Vauxhall Bridge Road, London SW1V 2SA

Random House Australia (Pty) Limited
20 Alfred Street, Milsons Point, Sydney,
New South Wales 2061, Australia

Random House New Zealand Limited
18 Poland Road, Glenfield, Auckland 10, New Zealand

Random House (Pty) Limited
Endulini, 5a Jubilee Road, Parktown 2193, South Africa

The Random House Group Limited Reg. No. 954009
www.randomhouse.co.uk

A CIP catalogue record for this book is available from the British Library

Papers used by Random House are natural,
recyclable products made from wood grown in sustainable forests.
The manufacturing processes conform to the environmental
regulations of the country of origin

ISBN 0 0994 3649 3

Design/Make up by Roger Walker

Printed and bound in Denmark by Nørhaven A/S, Viborg

Contents

David McKee

Tess Read

Author's Note

Red Knight was the first Mr Benn adventure, written as a book by David McKee and published by Dobson in 1967. After publication the BBC commissioned David to make a series for TV. David created 13 Mr Benn TV episodes, each 15 minutes long, comprising *Red Knight* and 12 new episodes. While the Mr Benn adventures were successfully running and re-running on BBC David turned two of the episodes into books – *Big Game Benn* (Hunter) (1979), and *Big Top Benn* (Clown) (1980). This last featured Smasher in the book, although not in the TV episode; the book version has been used. As it has for Hunter. (The book version features several hunters, the TV episode has only one). In addition, David wrote *123456789 Benn* (Prisoner) (published 1970), but this was never made into a TV episode because the BBC considered it too controversial. This year David has written a new Mr Benn book, *Gladiator* (Anderson Press, 2001) which has not yet been made for television.

In addition to the four original books, four Mr Benn books of the television series were published by Hodder and

Stoughton in 1993 using artwork not drawn by David. Two illustrations are reproduced here from these books – the man in rags in *Spaceman*, and cars and dinosaurs on Festive Road in *Caveman*.

All other illustrations reproduced in this book, with David and King Rollo Film's kind permission, come from the original books and *Gladiator*, from the television episodes, and from the very little of David's artwork created for the television episodes which he had not thrown on a Putney skip in the 1970s!

Acknowledgments

Great thanks go to Ron Beard for the idea, Clare Smith for her untiring competence, Roger Walker for his superb picture-craft, Graham Read for his thoughtful inspiration, Daniel Davies for his undying loveliness and, of course, David McKee for Mr Benn.

To Joe
For all your possible tomorrows

Mr Benn

Mr Benn leads a gentle life. The busy bustling world goes on outside his door in Festive Road where the street is always full of playing children. He steps out of his house at number 52, an ordinary bowler-hatted figure, but steps into the costume shop ready to do extraordinary things.

Whether he is transported to Roman times, plunged under the sea or launched into space there is always a puzzle to solve or a wrong to be righted. And whatever the problem, his way is always the same – kindness, thoughtfulness and compassion.

Keep life simple and you will get more from it.

Mr Benn visits the costume shop to have adventures. When he changes outfits he discovers another world and then transforms that world, changing it for the better by remedying injustices he finds. Always, he looks around him, listens, empathises and finds that progress is always possible.

The world is right for him when children are not hungry, prisoners are not mis-treated, animals are taken care of and cheats do not triumph. Ordinary Festive Road, where people are free and children are loved, is nearly perfect. So, in Festive Road, as in the wider world, everyone must take responsibility for everyone else's welfare. Society is all of us and we must take care of everyone, according to Mr Benn's liberal philosophy.

Mr Benn never forces change in his adventures. He may explain, flatter and trick, but he never bullies. Rather, he lets other people see the best course of action for themselves. And he never takes the credit – refusing point blank to let Smasher announce him as the initiator of the idea to put joy back in the prison. Indeed he never announces his departure: he just slips away.

Mr Benn's different costumes let him be different people. But he is always glad to return to his own clothes, his own self, and Festive Road. From each adventure he keeps a memento the shopkeeper gives him, displaying them all on his mantelpiece. And after each adventure the world has changed for the better, just a little, in Festive Road too, in celebration. The ordinary, anonymous-looking, plain-suited Mr Benn has brought out the best spirits of everyone, because he is the kindly part of all of us.

Mr Benn has only had 15 adventures in all – so far.

Ordinary life is extraordinarily special.
Cherish it.

Red Knight

MALICIOUS RUMOURS

Where Mr Benn finds that bad judgments are
made in haste, but repented at leisure

The story so far

It is Saturday morning in Festive Road. Coal is being delivered in great sacks and children are playing with wooden swords. The postman knocks on the door of number 52, Mr Benn's house, and hands him an invitation to a party, a fancy dress party. That could be fun, Mr Benn thinks. He must go and find himself a costume.

Mr Benn sets off for the shops, but everywhere he finds only day-to-day clothes. He is walking back home when he turns into a small lane and sees a shop with strange costumes in the window.

He particularly likes an outfit of red armour. He steps inside and the shopkeeper appears. Mr Benn asks if he can borrow the costume. "Of course," smiles the shopkeeper, and invites Mr Benn to try it on to see if it fits.

Mr Benn changes into the armour and admires his reflection in the mirror. He notices another door, not the one he came in by. "Well," he says to himself, and walks through. To his surprise he finds he has walked out into a strange rocky landscape.

He looks around and sees smoke rising from behind nearby boulders. There beneath the rocks is a huge green dragon. At first, Mr Benn thinks it is someone dressed up in a rather splendid costume, but then he realises it is a real dragon – a great, sad, weeping dragon.

He sits down next to the dragon and hears his tale. The dragon used to light fires for all the people in the kingdom. Everybody loved him, especially the King. But one day a man came to the realm selling things called matches. Of course nobody needed his matches so they didn't buy them. But the match-seller was canny: he burnt down a few barns and saw that the dragon was blamed. The dragon was hounded out of town, and had been hiding out here ever since. To make matters worse, the King's favourite horse had run away here and everybody thought the dragon had kidnapped him. The dragon was looking after him, but was much too afraid to take him back.

"Don't worry" says Mr Benn "I'll help you." They set off straight away for the King's castle. The dragon hides in some nearby trees and Mr Benn rides the horse to the castle gates.

As he nears the castle hundreds of people greet Mr Benn – they are sure he has slain the dragon and is returning the King's stolen horse triumphant. He is led directly to the King. But Mr Benn halts any congratulations and instead tells the King what has really happened.

The King is shocked and saddened. He sends for the match-seller and orders him thrown in the darkest dungeon, and then journeys out on foot with Mr Benn to apologise to the dragon. The dragon forgives the King and they all ride happily to the castle on the great creature's back. There shall be a feast in honour of the Red Knight to celebrate the dragon's return, announces the King.

Mr Benn watches with excitement as the banquet is prepared, until a small, strangely familiar man appears, and asks if he would like to follow him to change for the feast. To his surprise Mr Benn finds himself back in the shop, beside his own clothes.

"I think I've had enough excitement now," he tells the shopkeeper. "I don't think I'll go to the fancy dress party after all." The shopkeeper smiles. "Will we be seeing you again, Sir?" he says. "Oh yes", says Mr Benn.

Everything is as it always has been in Festive Road, except that Mr Benn finds in his pocket an unusual box of matches – decorated with a picture of a dragon.

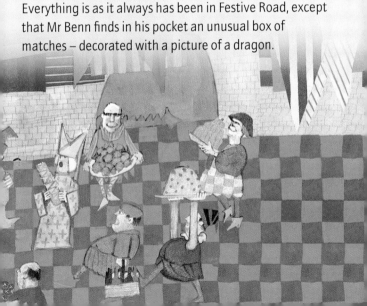

Good thinking, Mr Benn

Mr Benn doesn't know what lies behind the other door in the changing room. But he decides to venture out, into an adventure.

Take up challenges

The problem was
solved because of
listening – Mr Benn sat
down and listened to
the dragon's sad tale,
and the King listened to
Mr Benn's explanation.

Listen

Mr Benn is disappointed to find no shops selling interesting clothes, only many shops selling rack upon rack of similar clothes. He has to go somewhere quite out of the way for something rather out of the ordinary.

Search to express your individuality

The match-seller is well punished for his crimes. Not only is he thrown into the deepest dungeon with no hope of release, but the King also rules that he shall have to make matches for free for all the people of the Kingdom in perpetuity. Meanwhile the dragon is to be the King's personal fire-lighter.

Troublemakers can't always expect clemency

Once the dragon had been blamed for burning the barns it was but a small leap of the imagination to find him guilty of abducting the King's horse. In fact, of course, the dragon didn't steal the horse, but neither did the villainous match-seller. The horse simply ran away.

Don't assume every misfortune
has the same perpetrator

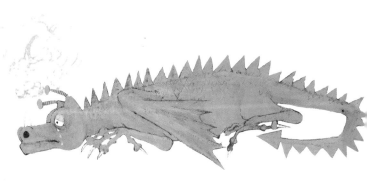

123456789 Benn
(Prisoner)

CREATIVITY

Where Mr Benn finds that nobody benefits
from harsh punishment

The story so far

Mr Benn wakes up one morning in Festive Road and takes a look around his room. He feels rather shut in by the four walls today. Perhaps he should go for a walk. His feet take him along the street, down the side-streets and into the little lanes. There he finds the costume shop and decides to look inside. He spots a costume covered in stripes with 123456789 stitched on. Just as he is wondering what to make of it, the shopkeeper invites him to try it on.

Mr Benn climbs into the outfit in the changing room, then notices another door and walks through.

The door clangs shut behind him and he finds himself facing a little barred window inside a small dark room. He looks through the window and sees hundreds of other barred windows set into big locked doors. Behind each window is a man looking out, and crying. He realises he is a prisoner in a big, unhappy prison.

There is a noise behind him and he turns around – to see a huge mean convict.

Is it because of you that all the men are crying, asks Mr Benn. "No" says Smasher, "It's this place. You'll see."

And Mr Benn does see. A bell rings for breakfast, but this horrible excuse for food is like no breakfast Mr Benn has ever had. And everyone cries into their tepid tea and onto their soggy toast making it taste even worse.

Then another bell rings, and the prisoners march along the grey, grey corridors to sew grey mailbags, or to make grey clothes, or to mix paint. The paint mixers take bright colours of paint and stir them together until the mix is grey. And all the while the convicts are crying. Even the guards look close to tears.

Mr Benn suggests to Smasher that if he is the boss perhaps he should try to make the prison more cheerful: the prisoners could paint with bright colours, cook better food, sew colourful uniforms. Smasher is astounded – he has never heard such a revolutionary idea. Well, he thinks, why not?

He taps the pipes in his cell and spreads the word around the prison. The convicts are flabbergasted; but they all take to the idea eagerly.

After lunch the prisoners rush to order colourful uniforms from the convict tailors and bright paint from the paint-mixers. The convict cooks hurry to the kitchen to prepare a special dinner. The guards are flummoxed by the commotion, let alone the occasional joyful singing. But they can't help liking the results.

All the prisoners are wearing brightly coloured uniforms and have painted their cells with different fantastical designs. There is no more crying, and guards and prisoners alike see the world with new eyes.

When the bell rings for dinner there is another treat in store – deliciously edible food. A familiar-looking guard approaches Mr Benn: "Prisoner 123456789, come with me". Mr Benn finds himself back in the shop.

Mr Benn walks back along Festive Road. It is good to be free, he thinks, although I should like to see Smasher again. Perhaps he will …

Good thinking, Mr Benn

Everyone has creativity

The guards were dumbfounded by the convicts' plans for the prison, but they had to admit the paintings and bright colours were a great improvement.

Allow people creative space

At first the guards complain that the brightly coloured uniforms the prisoners create are not allowed. But the uniform-makers point out the rule stipulates that uniforms must be striped, but specifies nothing about colours. The guards have to admit this is right. And they too prefer the vibrant colours to shades of grey.

If a rule is made it can be exploited

Over dinner in the evening with the prison cheered up, Smasher begins to get reconciled to life inside, but Mr Benn reminds him that he can do so much more free.

Freedom is life's greatest luxury

Caveman

RUSH HOUR

Where Mr Benn returns to the time of cavemen for a little peace and quiet, only to find that there has always been something trying to ruin your day

The story so far

Festive Road is unusually busy today. The main road is being repaired and all morning traffic crawls and honks its way past Mr Benn's door. So Mr Benn decides to go to the costume shop, in search of an adventure with some peace and quiet. He finds the caveman's costume and heads off to a land far away from the rush hour traffic. Or so he thinks.

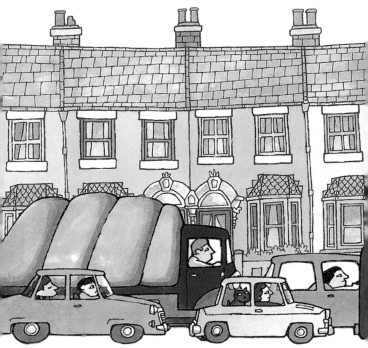

All is quiet outside the caves where the people live and Mr Benn stretches out on the grass and enjoys the sunshine,

but then he discovers why none of the people sheltering inside their caves are out on the grass with him….

Suddenly a cloud of approaching dust appears on the horizon, and he hears a rumble getting louder and louder. The cave people shout to warn Mr Benn who scurries out of the way of an approaching cavalcade of dinosaurs just in time.

Over breakfast with a cave family, Mr Benn discovers there is a rush of dinosaurs in the morning to get the best feeding places and a rush in the evening to get the best sleeping places. It's the bane of the cave people's lives. They can't step outside their caves without the risk of being crushed by a speeding dinosaur.

But surely, asks Mr Benn, there must be places to live that are not in the path of the dinosaur's daily routine? The cave people tell him that there certainly are and they take him for a walk to lovely fresh, green countryside and say that this is where they want to live.

"Why don't you, then?" asks Mr Benn. "Because there are no caves here, silly" is the reply. Mr Benn explains that they don't have to live in caves, they could build stone huts.

The cave people have never heard of such a thing and so Mr Benn sets about showing them how. Together they build fine stone huts with grass turf roofs. When all the work is done the delighted cave people climb a hill to watch the dinosaur rush hour safely from afar.

Then the shopkeeper appears and leads Mr Benn back into the shop.

Back in Festive Road the cars and lorries are still pushing and shoving their way along the little street and momentarily Mr Benn sees them as big lumbering dinosaurs. At his gate he finds a stone hammer in his pocket – it's just the thing to help him remember his adventure.

AS IF BY MAGIC

Good thinking, Mr Benn

Mr Benn finds the cave people living in caves, just as their name would suggest. But he has an idea which transforms their lives by taking them away from the dusty dangerous dinosaur route. Now they live next to a bubbling brook, and their homes are stone huts topped with green turf. The cave people did not have to live in caves, realised Mr Benn.

A name need not be a trap

In Festive Road Mr Benn tries to watch a TV programme about cavemen. Being an inquisitive soul he is interested to know about their lives, their furs and their stone tools, but he is too distracted by the noise of the traffic outside to learn much. So he gives up on the whole thing and decides to go out to the costume shop, determined to get away from all the noise.

In the shop he spies the caveman's costume and asks the shopkeeper about it. The shopkeeper also tells him about the cave people – but Mr Benn only really learns about them by stepping into their world.

We learn by doing, not by watching.

"He smiled at the furry Mr Benn in the mirror."

Mr Benn is going to become a caveman, not just visit them. After the cave people warn him about the stampeding dinosaurs, they invite him in and he spends the night in a cave, snuggled down in a bundle of furs. In the morning, he is woken by the cries of men trying to shift a dinosaur sitting in front of a cave entrance; he helps to move the great animal.

Fitting in brings the reward of acceptance

Mr Benn suggests that the cave people could make stone huts to be their homes instead of caves. They listen to his idea and, although they have never heard of such a thing, soon they are all collecting stones, chopping down wood and cutting turf. Their problem is solved by their willingness to listen to new ideas, even though what Mr Benn proposes is totally new to them.

Be open to new ideas

The dinosaurs are so impatient, complain the cave people, they are always in a rush. They are clumsy too – they don't mean any harm but if you are in the way they are likely to crash into you and their size makes them dangerous.

Back in Festive Road Mr Benn looks at the hooting cars still crawling along the street with dismay. For a moment he sees them as dinosaurs, and they seem to make more sense that way! It is almost as if their large and clumsy shapes let the drivers pretend they have brains the size of peas – their excuse for driving without enough respect or patience.

Machines should serve us, not change us

Balloonist

CHEATING

Where Mr Benn shows
that no good comes to
those who cheat

The story so far

Clouds drift gently above
Festive Road. But things aren't so
peaceful on the ground. Children
are playing noisily with balloons –
blowing them up and letting go. Mr
Benn looks at the children and up
again at the clouds – how lovely it
would be to float so freely in the sky.
He thinks of the costume shop...

In the shop Mr Benn picks out an outfit very like his own clothes. He admires the costume in the mirror – a brown double-breasted suit with a yellow tie finished off with a tall top hat – and walks through the door which leads to adventures.

He finds himself in a large crowd, awaiting the start of a balloon race. One of the six balloons has only one person in its basket – a forlorn young man who tells Mr Benn that they are going to race to the next town but it is hard to win against a cheat. "A cheat?" queries Mr Benn. "Baron Bartrum" replies the young man.

BARON
BARTRUM

The young man thinks the Baron is behind the non-appearance of his co-balloonist: he can't do the race alone. Mr Benn offers to take his place and the young man is delighted. Seconds later the race begins.

But not very far – Mr Benn's balloon has been tied to the drainpipe of a house and now it is stuck. Mr Benn yanks the drainpipe and the balloon comes free, dangling the drainpipe behind it. The other balloonists have not been so lucky – all their balloons have contraptions attached to them which have been sabotaged by Baron Bartrum.

One balloon has a kite attached to pull it along, but now the kite is just pulling the balloon upwards.

One has a propellor but it has been turned backwards and the balloon is going in the wrong direction.

A balloon with two sails has lost one of the sails so the balloon just turns around in circles.

And one balloon has oars for the balloonists to pull on. But the Baron has cunningly covered the oars with bird seed…

Only two balloons – the Baron's and Mr Benn's – float up and away. They gently move through the sky, high above the green trees and the lush fields.

It's lovely to be up among the clouds, thinks Mr Benn, and his balloon sails past the Baron's. But the Baron has another trick up his sleeve.

Suddenly he drops a rope as he flies over a wood below, his companion blows a horn and a man on a horse appears and attaches the end of the rope to the saddle of the horse which gallops ahead, pulling the balloon with it. Now it's his turn to overtake Mr Benn.

But the race isn't over yet. Mr Benn and his companion let some gas out of the balloon and funnel it into the drainpipe. It works! As they let gas out, the balloon loses a little height, but with the drainpipe stuck out behind it is propelled forwards more quickly.

They overtake the Baron's balloon and the noise of the escaping gas startles the horse, who throws off its rider, turns tail, and drags the Baron's balloon back towards the wood – in completely the wrong direction.

Mr Benn and his companion win the race by a long way. Mr Benn's companion is awarded a gold cup by the town's mayor, and the shopkeeper leads Mr Benn away to give him his medal.

Back in Festive Road children are still playing with balloons but now they have tied the balloons with string – so they drift above the children's heads.

Good thinking, Mr Benn

Baron Bartrum so wanted to win.
He was always thinking of the
moment of victory, of the prize
being presented to him.

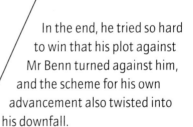

In the end, he tried so hard
to win that his plot against
Mr Benn turned against him,
and the scheme for his own
advancement also twisted into
his downfall.

If you set a petard
you may be hoist with it

As Mr Benn's companion sees the Baron's trick with the horse he loses all hope of winning the race. The odds are stacked against them – surely they have no chance against someone who cheats so often, and so well. But Mr Benn is not disheartened. He looks around him, and – what luck! The drainpipe that the Baron had tried to fix them to would actually help them win. Startling the Baron's horse so that it fled with the Baron's balloon in the wrong direction was a happy accident.

You make your own luck

Mr Benn loved the tranquillity of the balloon flight. He felt like a cloud, far above the bustle of everyday life. He wasn't there just to race, but to enjoy the ride.

Enjoy the means and the ends may come

When Mr Benn stepped out of the changing room he found himself at the back of a crowd. He worked his way to the front and saw the six balloons – five with two men in the basket and one with just one. Mr Benn asked the young man if he could ride with him – the young man was pleased to say yes.

Ask people if they might need your help, you cannot assume they will ask you

Before the balloons set off Mr Benn was surprised to see that all the others except for the Baron's had speed-enhancing devices added to them. The Baron, of course, had a device of his own later in the race – the horse.

But none of the contraptions helped the balloonists at all. Only Mr Benn's balloon was a plain balloon. It seems that the more attachments each balloon had, the more things there were to go wrong.

Don't over-technologise

Hunter

FLATTERY

Where Mr Benn finds that vain people
are so easy to trick

The story so far

It is another ordinary day in Festive Road. Neighbours are looking at plants and children are chasing cats. Mr Benn decides to go for a walk. He passes a pet shop and a florist and then recognises the lane where the unusual costume shop is. He steps inside, and wonders what would be in keeping with all the animals and plants he has been seeing. "A hunter's costume, Sir?" suggests the shopkeeper, and he points Mr Benn in the direction of the changing room.

Mr Benn changes into the outfit, ventures out through the other door of the changing room, and finds himself emerging from a tent into the jungle. He barely has time to look around before a man dressed like him addresses him as the new guide and tells him to lead the way to the big game hunting.

Mr Benn takes the news well and begins leading the hunters through trails in the jungle. But he finds their guns rather alarming and really doesn't want any of the wildlife to be on the receiving end of bullets.

The hunters follow him through the jungle, all the while boasting how they are the world's greatest big game hunters. "Let me prove it to you" says a hunter, and takes aim at a tiny bird. But surely, Mr Benn protests, the best big game hunters are not interested in such small fry. "Oh, quite, no" says the hunter, and pretends to have only been adjusting his sights rather than aiming at the diminutive creature.

They round a bend and come upon a deer atop a hill. "Ah" says the hunter. But, no, no, says Mr Benn, not large enough.

Then they stalk their way around a giraffe.

"He's tall," says Mr Benn, "but not fat enough."

And so Mr Benn goes on finding every animal not quite big enough, dissuading the hunters from shooting at a crocodile, a hippo and a lion. The frustrated hunters sit down to have their lunch and a nap. Mr Benn goes for a walk, something was worrying him. He has saved the animals so far, but …

He turns a corner and suddenly the ground starts shaking. In front of him is a huge herd of trembling elephants, shuddering with fear. For they are the largest animals in the forest and how is he to save them?

Mr Benn sees the problem. He has a think, he has a plan.

He explains it to the elephants.

Mr Benn rushes back to the men and hurries them along –
he has found animals large enough for such talented
hunters. He leads them straight to the elephants, the
hunters raise their sights with glee, then at Mr Benn's
signal the elephants jump up and down, shaking the
jungle floor, and causing all the hunters' bullets to fly into
the air or embed themselves in the ground.

Mr Benn looks shocked – he is ashamed of such poor
hunters. They are not safe with guns. Perhaps they should
try shooting things with cameras instead.

They return to the tent and a man selling cameras
suddenly appears.

He leads Mr Benn into the tent and Mr Benn finds himself back in the shop. The shopkeeper hands Mr Benn a photograph of a whole herd of elephants. It seems the hunters were better at taking pictures after all.

Mr Benn has enjoyed his adventure but he is happy to be back in Festive Road where children are taking photographs and all is well with the world.

Good thinking, Mr Benn

Mr Benn strings the hunters along all day by repeating the mantra that the animal they are aiming at is not enough of a challenge.

Don't change a winning strategy

Mr Benn does not see in advance how to save the elephants. But he keeps on with his plan, trusting to luck that something will turn up, as indeed it does.

There is always hope around the corner

The elephants are the biggest and most powerful animals in the jungle. Nevertheless they were petrified by the hunters and their guns.

Everyone has feelings

Spaceman

THE GRASS IS ALWAYS GREENER

Where Mr Benn finds out that you should value
what you have because perfection is unattainable

Festive Road is as busy as ever. Mr Benn is not in his house at number 52, he is in the garden talking with his neighbour. They are discussing the relative merits of one another's lawn – surely the other's is more green and lush, they each say.

Mr Benn takes a stroll in the park, and when he sees a kite soaring up into the blue beyond, his mind turns to the possibilities of adventures in space. He walks to the costume shop and immediately picks out a spaceman's outfit. "I do believe you have made up your mind, Sir." says the shopkeeper.

Mr Benn steps into the changing room, climbs into the outfit and ventures out through the other door. Into … a spaceship! "Ready for blast off?" says another spaceman at the controls. "Here we go!"

The spaceship zooms up into the air and then settles into a gentle climb. Mr Benn looks out of the craft's window and marvels at the multitude of stars and planets they are passing by. For the first time he wonders where they are headed. To a planet of gold and jewels, the spaceman tells him. "We are going to be rich." That could be nice, thinks Mr Benn.

The spaceship lands and Mr Benn and the spaceman step out onto a miraculous planet encrusted with gold, silver and precious jewels as far as the eye can see. They are filling their arms with the dazzling treasure when they come across a man in rags sitting dejected on a lump of gold. The stones are worthless, he tells them, for they change into base metal the moment they leave the planet's atmosphere.

"It's the next planet you want – they have everything there, and it's all free."

Mr Benn and the spaceman don't need to be told twice.
They get straight back into the spaceship, land on the
next planet and find themselves in a paradise of
consumerism. There are shops, cafes, all brimming with
goods, and everything is free.

They sit down in a restaurant. But there's something
wrong here ....

Everything is black and white! Yes, the restaurateur tells them, this planet has no colour, and if you stay here for long you will lose your colour too. It's the next planet you need.

The planet-hopping duo are back in their spaceship within minutes. At the next planet, they resolve to be cautious. They peer out of the spaceship's window, everything appears fine – all the people have strange hats on their heads, but that's obviously just fashion.

They step outside, and .. a terrible cacophony assaults their ears – like a hundred brass bands playing.

Mr Benn and the spaceman hurry back into the spaceship. Now the spaceman is lost and needs to land on another planet to find the way. At the next planet, which appears delightful but turns out to be dreadfully hot, there is a man ready to give the spaceman directions.

"I think I'll stay here," says Mr Benn. "I've had enough of travelling." The man leads Mr Benn into a cave, to be cool and Mr Benn finds himself back in the shop. He asks the shopkeeper where he sent the spaceman "Here, Sir. Back to earth. It's not perfect, but it's not too bad either."

Good thinking, Mr Benn

Mr Benn wanted to travel into space just to see what it was like, but the exploration turned into a mission as he became waylaid by thoughts of becoming rich.

Preserve your values

When Mr Benn returned to Festive Road he found in his pocket a stone from the bejewelled planet. It had turned to dark green and nobody would believe it had ever been bright shining gold. But he thought it was beautiful, and it was just the thing to help him remember.

Treasure things precious to you

Gold and jewels which cannot be exchanged for the real riches of life – food, warmth, comfort – are worthless, as the man in rags knew only too well.

Value the important things in life

Mr Benn and the spaceman wanted to change their world, but only in certain ways. They couldn't imagine a life without colour, but when they experienced it they were horrified.

You cannot cherry-pick change

The quiet of this world was something Mr Benn and the spaceman had never truly noticed. Until all around them was discordant cacophony.

Appreciate the life you have

Cook

FRIENDSHIP

Where Mr Benn shows that no one
will thank you for spoiling someone you love
at the expense of others

The story so far

It's a quiet morning in Festive Road, until a sweet-sounding tune tinkles down the street and an ice cream van pulls up. Children gather excitedly to buy icelollies. Mr Benn decides to go for a walk to the costume shop where adventures start from.

In the shop the shopkeeper smiles when Mr Benn picks out a long white buttoned tunic with a tall chef's hat. Mr Benn goes into the changing room, buttons himself into the costume and steps into …

A dark dingy street of tall thin houses where small thin children crouch in doorways, huddling together for warmth and comfort. Mr Benn is wondering what to do when ahead of him he sees cooks dressed as he is all heading off somewhere. He follows.

The collection of cooks walk through the city, up to the gates of a Palace, past the guards and into the Palace's kitchen, where hundreds of cooks are already busy – cooking and basting, roasting and tasting. What can it all be for, wonders Mr Benn. And then he finds out.

Each time a cook has finished a dish a fanfare is sounded and the cook proudly bears the delight into a great hall where sits a concerned King, a distressed Queen and in between them a bored, grumpy, uninterested little Princess, Annabella. And whatever the dish laid before her, and however much her parents extol its virtues, Annabella does not eat. She will not eat.

Each time, her parents send the dish back mournfully to a growing mound of uneaten delicacies and the next cook tries their luck. But it is always in vain.

"Excuse me" Mr Benn says to a servant. "I have an idea, if the King will let me try it." "Anything!" exclaims the exasperated King.

Mr Benn tells the cooks to prepare for a banquet, rushes out of the Palace, runs down the streets of the city and finds the poor hungry children. "There's to be a feast at the Palace and you are all invited." He returns to the Palace with the ragged and bedraggled hungry children, takes them into the imposing hall, where the table is now piled high with fantastic foods, and tells them to help themselves.

The children cannot believe their luck, and feast their eyes on the gorgeous fare. Then they tuck in. A boy offers Annabella a plate of cakes. The King and Queen hold their breaths. She takes one, then another. And soon she is eating and laughing with all the other children. "Can they come back next week?" she asks the King. "Of course, my dear, they can come every week."

A man appears and asks Mr Benn to take a spoon into the kitchen. He finds himself back in the shop. He thanks the shopkeeper and with a smile walks home to Festive Road. The children here aren't hungry.

Good thinking, Mr Benn

See Annabella smile at the feast.

Children need the company of other children

Nothing can make you quite as happy
as making other people happy

Everybody in the Palace was too busy preparing the next nice meal which Annabella might eat, to think about possible alternative ideas.

Change a losing strategy

It is less easy to be wilful or spoilt when confronted with genuine need.

Facing real want leads to self-understanding

Annabella has her reasons for not eating,
and no amount of her parents asking, cajoling, or
telling her to eat will make her. Indeed, there is nothing
more likely to put you off your food than being fussed
over, stared at, and ordered to eat.

Try to understand problems not alter behaviour

Magic Carpet

FREEDOM

Where Mr Benn shows
that you should
not let people
slave for you,
even if they
offer to.

The story so far

It is a sunny morning in Festive Road and people are coming and going as usual. There is a man dressed in exotic clothes trying to sell a carpet. It reminds Mr Benn of the costume shop and he goes for a walk in search of a new outfit and a new adventure.

"Good morning" says the shopkeeper. "Do you see something you would like to try on?" "Is there a carpet with this one?" Mr Benn jokes. Ah yes, replies the shopkeeper, rather a special carpet. Mr Benn takes the costume into the changing room to try it for size. Then he steps out of the other door, the one that leads to adventures.

Mr Benn finds himself surrounded by sand, nothing but desert-yellow sand. He lays the carpet down and sits on it – time for a think. The carpet begins to move. Of course! – it's a magic carpet.

The carpet carries Mr Benn above the sand and sets him down at the gates of a town. The town is beautiful – all white-washed buildings and minarets. Children are playing around a fountain, but one small boy is yanked away. Mr Benn watches, concerned, as a man drags the boy to the edge of town where he tells him to squeeze into a small cave entrance and retrieve a green bottle.

The boy unwillingly squirms his way inside the cave and emerges with a bottle. The man makes to grab the bottle but before he can take hold of it a great bird swoops down and carries it to the top of a tall pile of rocks. The man crossly tells the boy to fetch it and bring it to him in the town. "Let me help" offers Mr Benn when the man has gone, and together they fly up on the carpet to the bottle.

"I wonder what's in the bottle" says Mr Benn. The boy undoes the stopper and they find out.

"I am the genie of the bottle. I can do anything and I obey
you who has let me out."

"What would you like me to do?" asks the genie. The boy
asks the genie to go back into the bottle while he has a
think. Perhaps, he wonders, the genie could build him
somewhere away from the town to live. So Mr Benn invites
the boy back on the magic carpet and they search for the
right place.

Beyond the town the boy opens the stopper again and asks the genie to build a Palace, surrounded with flowers and trees. A beautiful Palace springs up in the desert. Mr Benn and the boy marvel at it, but then the boy wonders what he is to do – for if he lives here he will miss his friends, but if he returns to the town the man will make him hand over the bottle and the genie will be in his command.

Mr Benn has an idea.

The boy asks the genie to make a cave near the town, fill it with identical green bottles and take them there. In an instant they are at the cave and when the boy has fetched the man they watch him search in vain amongst all the bottles. They know he will never find the one he wants.

Then the boy gives the bottle to the genie.

"Now you belong to yourself, and the Palace can be yours to live in."

The boy skips away to join his friends and a man appears and leads Mr Benn away. He knows what to expect.

Back in the shop he thanks the shopkeeper. "I do enjoy my visits." "Thank you, Sir. Shall we see you again soon?" the shopkeeper asks.

Children are playing in Festive Road as Mr Benn walks to his house at number 52. Scrabbling for the doorkey in his pocket he finds instead the stopper from the bottle. Just the thing to help him remember.

Good thinking, Mr Benn

The boy had no loyalty to the man because he had been ill-treated by him. So it was reckless for the man to leave the boy on his own to fetch the bottle from the top of the rocks – once the boy had the bottle he had no reason to bring it back to the man.

Lead by inclusion, don't rule by fear

Mr Benn and the boy wanted to prevent the genie from being at the man's beck and call, but Mr Benn saw that the best way to avoid this was not to allot him a more worthy master but to give him his liberty.

Freedom is the greatest gift

The boy realised that he did not want somewhere so grand or ostentatious to live in as a Palace. He would be happy just to be near his friends in his town.

Home is where the heart is

Clown

ACTING THE FOOL

Where Mr Benn finds that everyone
can do something

The story so far

Children are playing on Festive Road and Mr Benn can
hear the sound of laughter. He looks out of his window
and sees a girl juggling, while another has on a funny
mask and he thinks what fun it must be to make people
laugh. He sets off for the costume shop and a clown's
costume with a bright red nose.

The shopkeeper suggests he try it on, he would love to. He
changes into the outfit and looks at the reflection in the
mirror – he even makes himself chuckle.

Then he galumphs with his
huge shoes out through the
other door, it will lead to a
circus ring he supposes.

But no, he is out in open countryside – nothing but trees, fields … and a bright little car. It must surely be for him.

Mr Benn drives off in the funny little car, wondering what will happen next, then he rounds a bend, sees a great collection of people and brightly painted vehicles, and suddenly the car does a rattle and a squeak and a  bump and with a bang lands Mr Benn in the middle of them all. The troupe laugh and ask if he would like to join their circus – they could use another clown.

So here is the circus – Mr Benn is delighted – but why, he wonders are they in the middle of the countryside. Then he sees a mass of boulders at the head of the line of vehicles: a landslide is blocking the road. Beyond is the town where the company is due to perform this evening, but how are they to get there? Mr Benn sets off across the fields to get help and sees a large man over the brow of a hill – Smasher Lagru from the prison!

Smasher has a hard time recognising Mr Benn until he takes off his red nose, then he gives Mr Benn a hearty clap on the back. He has been let out of prison and is in search of an honest job. Huge tough Smasher might be just the thing, thinks Mr Benn.

The circus people are disappointed to see Mr Benn return with only one man, admittedly a hefty one, but their spirits rise when they see the alacrity with which Smasher takes to lifting, smashing and clearing the rocks. In fact they are so impressed that they offer Smasher the job of strongman with them. Smasher grins a big toothy grin.

But when all the stones are cleared, the circus vehicles come to another grinding halt. The ringmaster mournfully gazes at a huge gap in the road ahead of them where a bridge over the fast-flowing river had been.

Then everyone starts talking at once. They all have different ideas how to get across – Smasher wants to put rocks in and walk across, but that would stop the flow of the river says Mr Benn. The stiltwalker wants to make stilts for everyone, but that is no good for the trucks, says Mr Benn. The conjurer wants to conjure them all across, but nobody thinks that is safe.

Then Mr Benn makes a suggestion – they all work together to make a bridge. They get straight to work, each helping in different ways, and soon the bridge is made.

The troupe arrive in the next town and Mr Benn watches the evening's show. He wonders at the gravity-defying tightrope walkers, the trapeze artists who swing through the air, the extraordinary strength of Smasher, and the brilliance of a magician who looks awfully familiar. Mr Benn then drives in his little clown car – it squeaks and bumps and flings him on the ground. The audience love him.

The magician invites him into a magic cabinet and Mr Benn finds himself back in the shop.

"You're a very good magician" he says to the shopkeeper. "Everyone can do something, Sir" says the shopkeeper.

Back in Festive Road the children are still playing, and laughing.

Good thinking, Mr Benn

Mr Benn acts the clown in front of the circus people, yet he is listened to when he suggests building a bridge to cross the river. The troupe understand him as a 3-dimensional person with a silly and a serious side.

You need not be serious at all times
to be taken seriously sometimes

Mr Benn when faced with the landslide in the road and the bridge that isn't there knows that individual solutions will not work – the circus needs to work together as a team.

Work together using everyone's abilities to the full

The circus troupe always put up the big top together, and create each show together. But they couldn't see that they could build a bridge through working together until Mr Benn suggested it to them.

An outsider may see the solution you cannot

How nice, thinks Mr Benn, to be able to make people laugh. People laugh at his clown – he is prepared to make himself look silly and that is funny. So he plays at being silly, just as the children do.

Play enriches us all

Mr Benn's clown car acts very peculiarly when there are people around. When he is alone is looks bright and eccentric but drives straight. So Mr Benn has a performing side of him which appears when he is in the company of others and not otherwise. This does not make him two-faced or not himself, but is the usual countenance of comedy.

To perform in front of others is natural

Diver

PEARLS OF WISDOM

Where Mr Benn dives deep and finds that
you should enjoy life as you go along,
not search for a single prize

The story so far

The sun is shining in Festive Road and children are listening to sea-shells. Mr Benn is at the riverside, watching the boats go by. The water seems to hold a world of adventures in it and it turns Mr Benn to thinking of the costume shop. He goes to the shop and finds a red frogman's outfit. Perfect – he will dive under the sea and explore this watery world.

Mr Benn walks out of the changing room and onto a rocky shoreline. He climbs onto a stony promontory and prepares to dive underwater. But just as he is about to plunge into the sea, sailors from a red submarine call out to him – they are going underwater to win the race to photograph the monster! He doesn't really have time to reply before sailors from a green submarine call out to him – they are anxious to let him know that they will be the first to see the monster and take its photograph.

Mr Benn is not looking for any monster so he just dives into the sea and is plunged into the beautiful aqua landscape under the waves. He swims and floats among the gliding fish and sea-horses bobbing up and down where water plants waft in the swell. And everything is quiet here, except for a chugging noise.

He had almost forgotten about the submarines. He dives down deeper to escape the noise and twists and turns to swim among a big shoal of fish. And then, quite to his surprise, he comes across a mermaid, and even more surprisingly she is listening to sea-shells.

The mermaid says hello and tells Mr Benn that she is listening to all the different sounds that shells make because she wants to find a new sound to give to King Neptune for his birthday. Mr Benn offers to help and soon they are combing the bottom of the sea for the shell with the best new sound. After a bit, Mr Benn finds a black and yellow shell which quite definitely makes the noise of a buzzing bee. The mermaid is delighted – King Neptune certainly does not have that one – and together they swim to the King's underwater cave to give him the gift.

King Neptune smiles at the birthday present, but he is not a happy King. Next to him sits a splendid pink creature who also looks miserable. It is the submarines, the King explains, they are forever cutting through the sea looking for his monster to photograph and it is such a nuisance because it means that the King and the monster can't go out.

Mr Benn sympathises, and then has an idea. He swims up to the surface and finds, as he expects, the green submarine filled with freshly-disappointed sailors from their latest fruitless trip underwater. Their quest has been in vain? He sympathises, and then makes a suggestion. They are probably scaring off the monster by looking so like, well, a submarine. Whereas if they dressed up the craft to look like a fellow monster, the real monster might be less camera-shy. The sailors love the plan and straight away set to work.

Of course, on the other side of a stony promontory Mr Benn comes across the red submarine, and they take to the plan just as enthusiastically.

Mr Benn dives in the sea and sweeps up King, monster and mermaid to witness the inevitable as the submarines motor around taking photographs of each other.

The King is delighted – the waters will be his again – and they all ride triumphantly on the monster's back to the shore. As Mr Benn waves them goodbye he sees the red submarine surfacing whilst proudly brandishing a photograph, and in the other direction the green submarine emerges, also flaunting monster snaps.

The shopkeeper appears and leads Mr Benn into a cave and he finds himself back in the changing room.

Back in Festive Road people are coming and going; a group of children are singing happy birthday and looking at presents.

Good thinking, Mr Benn

The mermaid tells Mr Benn that sea-shells don't all sound like the sea, rather they have different sounds. Mr Benn has not heard this before, but he is ready to believe it.

Accept new ideas

Mr Benn played a trick on the sailors not because he disapproved of what they were trying to do, but because in doing it they were being a nuisance.

Real freedom is liberty at no-one's expense

When Mr Benn finds himself back in the shop, the shopkeeper sees a shell stuck to the diving suit and gives it to Mr Benn as a keepsake. Back in Festive Road Mr Benn takes the momento out of his pocket and puts it to his ear. He loves the sound the shell makes, although he can't quite be sure what it is.

Beautiful sounds are in the ear of the beholder

Cowboy

PLAY

Where Mr
Benn shows
that rivalries
can be
played out
in games,
not acted
out with
violence

THE STORY SO FAR

Festive Road is thronging with blood-curdling cries and triumphal shouts today – the children are playing cowboys and Indians. Mr Benn is reading about a cowboy film at the cinema. He decides to take a stroll to see it. But there is such a queue at the cinema that he has a better idea – the costume shop and a cowboy outfit. The shopkeeper happily hands Mr Benn the costume and invites him to try it on.

Mr Benn steps into the changing room and out into a red and dust-brown barren landscape. He looks around him and sees smoke signals rising from a nearby outcrop of rocks. Then he spots a huddle of wigwams in the distance – the Indian settlement. He decides to take a closer look.

Mr Benn walks cautiously towards the painted wigwams and then begins to hear something – drums, beating out an insistent rhythm, and voices chanting.

Indians are gathered around a tall totem pole, and they are crying "Redskins, Redskins, we'll beat the cowboys today." A war dance – Mr Benn must warn the cowboys!

He sees a stray horse and races it to the cowboy town. He rides past the saloon and church and at the sheriff's house he fires his gun in the air and calls out that the Indians are coming! The sheriff emerges looking unconcerned. Yes, he knows they are coming. And yes, they are probably right that they will win. Mr Benn is horrified. But it is a good game, says the sheriff. A game? And then the sheriff explains.

Every week the cowboys and the Indians play a game of hide and seek against each other. One cowboy hides and one Indian hides while all the others count up to 100. It is good fun, but the Indians always win – the cowboys can never find the hidden Indian. Mr Benn asks if he can play and the sheriff happily agrees; Mr Benn can be the cowboy to hide.

Soon the Indians arrive and with the Indian chief
and the cowboy sheriff ready as judges, the game
begins. Mr Benn climbs up a red rocky cliff to hide.
But from the top he realises his footprints clearly lead
straight to the rocks. He sees a wood and thinks again. At
the wood he climbs up a tree and swings to the next, and
the next, until he grapples and clambers his way to the
other side all above ground.

Now he is not far from the Indians' encampment –
they will never think of looking for him there.
Still they might find him by his footprints.
        But not if ...

… he takes off his shoes and walks backwards.

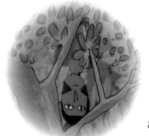

In the Indian encampment Mr Benn quickly hides in a wigwam. Meanwhile, the Indians are searching for him in the wood – they saw his footprints going in and there are none going out, so he must be there. But they cannot find him.

From his hiding place Mr Benn hears the cowboys, they are walking around in the settlement looking for the Indian, but finding nothing. He peeks out from his hiding place, sees the cowboys, and the totem pole. It looks even taller than before.

Then he realises…

… the Indian is sitting on top of it.

But the cowboys can't see the Indian, until they hear stifled giggling, and suddenly a laugh rings out above them. Mr Benn has attached a feather to a long pole and is tickling the Indian. The cowboys fall about laughing; the Indians hear the commotion and come in from the wood. They see the feather, the Indian, the cowboys and they hoot with laughter too.

Mr Benn emerges from the wigwam and, amid the laughter, the sheriff congratulates and thanks him for making the cowboys win for the first time – he gives him his sheriff's badge as a prize. Mr Benn asks the Indians if they would do a victory dance and everyone celebrates.

Then the shopkeeper appears and when Mr Benn shows him his hiding place he finds himself back in the shop.

Back in Festive Road, the children are still playing – now they are playing hide and seek.

Good thinking, Mr Benn

Mr Benn finds the totem pole that he comes across in the Indian settlement dazzling – it is the first he has ever seen. Although it is totally unfamiliar to him he regards it closely enough to notice when he sees it later, that it is taller – taller to the tune of one man.

Take in detail to understand the big picture

Mr Benn wins the game not by announcing victory, but by letting the cowboys see the resolution for themselves.

Show a solution, don't describe it

Mr Benn's feather is a real rib-tickler which everyone laughs at, so defusing what could have been a nasty situation as the Indians discover they have lost for the first time.

There is nothing so infectious as laughter

Mr Benn wanted to watch a film about cowboys, but then he realises that he can *be* a cowboy instead. Not just through the magic of the costume shop, but also through playing a game.

Don't dream it, be it

Of course, children always know this. It is only adults who are queuing up to watch the film – the children are playing at cowboys and Indians and hide and seek in Festive Road.

Pirate

TREASURE

Where Mr Benn finds that beautiful things in
nature are as valuable as gold and jewels

The story so far

It's a stormy morning in Festive Road. Mr Benn waits for the pelting rain to stop and the skies to clear and then goes for a walk. To the costume shop, he thinks.

In the shop he lets fate decide which costume to try – he just spins around and points. The shopkeeper's eyes twinkle and Mr Benn takes the intriguing costume into the changing room. Could it be a pirate's outfit?

Sure enough, when Mr Benn steps out of the other door, he finds himself on the deck of a sailing ship and from the top of its mast is flying the skull and crossbones. Suddenly there is a cry of "Ship ahoy!" and bulky, bluff Captain Tempest appears from beneath deck. He orders the sailors to catch the ship they have spied and plunder its booty.

Mr Benn wonders at this. Can you catch the ship? he questions the sailors. They reply that they certainly could, but certainly won't. They are determined not to be pirates and haven't caught a ship yet. So it proves with this particular ship.

Mr Benn takes dinner into the Captain's quarters where he finds the Captain poring over a map of an island. His island, the Captain tells Mr Benn. But, he adds mournfully, there aren't any crosses on it because they haven't bagged any treasure to bury.

The ship pulls into harbour at the island – just in time, because a storm suddenly whips up. But "Ship ahoy!" rings out the cry again and the sailors turn to see a ship out at sea being tossed and turned by the great waves of the storm. The ship shall surely be wrecked if no-one saves her, say the sailors, but there is nothing they can do about it: the Captain would not permit a rescue. Mr Benn conspiratorially suggests to the sailors that they pretend to go after the ship for its treasure and really bring it back to harbour, and safety.

Mr Benn hauls down and hides the skull and crossbones while the sailors heave and strain, and soon they have rescued the ship and brought vessel and crew to the haven of harbour.

The Captain is delighted – so his sailors are not hopeless after all. The men of the rescued ship cheer Captain Tempest and his crew and the Captain is flattered, and pleased. Then remembers he is a pirate. "Of course, we only rescued you to steal your treasure" he thunders. "So hand it over. What is it? Gold? Jewels?"

The rescued sailors laugh – where is the ship's skull and crossbones if it is a pirate ship? And anyway, they have no treasure, only trees and flowers; but they will gladly give some of these to the Captain.

The Captain is highly distressed, until Mr Benn makes a suggestion. Why not plant trees on the island and mark each spot with a cross on the island's map. They can be treasure trees. The crew look hopefully at the Captain, will he agree? He beams, and Captain and crew are finally of the same mind – pirates no more.

A sailor plays an old sea-shanty and both crews join in lustily.

Then the shopkeeper appears and leads Mr Benn away from the happy scene. Back in the shop he finds the Jolly Roger flag still tucked under his tunic. "Captain Tempest won't be needing that any more, Sir, thanks to your help," says the shopkeeper, and offers the flag to Mr Benn. The largest souvenir yet.

Back in Festive Road it is sunny and warm now, and a fruit van is making deliveries.

Good thinking, Mr Benn

The Captain was not a pirate at ease with himself. In truth he was pleased to have rescued the ailing ship and delighted with his treasure of trees. Being mean and vicious was good for the image, but didn't do much for his soul.

Be your real self

Captain Tempest wanted treasure for his island because that's what pirates are meant to have. But his sailors didn't want to steal for their riches and in the end sailors and Captain alike were more than happy for their treasure to be trees.

Everything has the value you accord it

Captain Tempest's crew were daily fighting against the problem of being told to rob ships and having to trick the Captain out of it. They had no plan for how to prevent this happening in the future, but by keeping on trying, and by being true to themselves they chanced upon the solution. They just had to stick to their guns, or rather lack of them.

Look after the small picture and the big picture will look after itself

The captain kept telling the sailors they were useless because of their persistent failure to catch ships, but they knew they were good sailors really and were quite content to put up with this permanent jibe in exchange for not having to steal for treasure.

Have confidence in your own ability

Wizard

WISHING FOR CHANGE

Where Mr Benn spells out that it is not how things look that matter, but how they are

The story so far

Mr Benn looks out of his window at number 52 Festive Road and sees children and their parents are walking to the park. He follows to find out why. There is a magic show at the park, Mr Benn discovers, and as he watches the display he thinks of a certain shop.

In the costume shop Mr Benn finds a starry, glittery costume and the shopkeeper appears and invites him to try it on to see how well it fits.

Mr Benn steps out of the changing room and finds himself in a cavern packed with shelves from floor to ceiling and on every shelf is crammed books, jars, packets and other intriguing sundry. He is just studying a book called "Useful Spells" when in walk two men from the Palace. They have been sent to find a wizard – will he come with them? Mr Benn is happy to oblige and soon they are all clip-clopping their way through lovely countryside on a horse-drawn carriage.

People wave as they pass and everyone looks remarkably happy: "Oh they are happy" says Mr Benn's companion. "Our King is a good King, everybody loves him."

At the Palace Mr Benn is led into the great hall where a great many worried people are gathered. At the head of the hall sit a King and Queen. The Queen is an impressive stately woman. The King is a short happy man. This is a problem.

As the Queen sees it, the King is just not Kingly enough. For a start, he is too placid: "He should jump about more." Could Mr Benn cast a spell to make this happen? Mr Benn consults his book, says the appropriate spell, waves a magic wand and sure enough the King begins to jump about all over the floor, rather like a frog.

Stop! commands the Queen. That isn't what she has in mind at all. Mr Benn quickly finds the spell to reverse the charm.

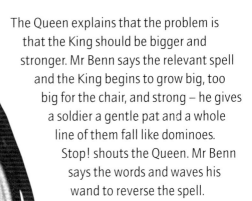

The Queen explains that the problem is that the King should be bigger and stronger. Mr Benn says the relevant spell and the King begins to grow big, too big for the chair, and strong – he gives a soldier a gentle pat and a whole line of them fall like dominoes. Stop! shouts the Queen. Mr Benn says the words and waves his wand to reverse the spell.

Perhaps strong is not right, suggests the Queen, but a King should certainly be tall and elegant, and she orders Mr Benn to make him so. Mr Benn reads the spell for height and elegance and the King begins to grow and grow.

The Queen calls out stop just before her King reaches the ceiling, and Mr Benn reverses the spell.

Exasperated, the Queen tries to make the King more statuesque. But, of course, he turns into stone. She tries to explain to Mr Benn that she ...but Mr Benn cuts her short. "Things cannot be changed to and fro forever" he says, and he refuses to cast another spell.

The Queen begs him to work one more charm, to reverse the spell and bring the King back to normal: "It's not important how he looks, I realise that now." Mr Benn reverses the spell and the Queen and crowd rejoice. The King smiles and thanks Mr Benn.

Back in the shop Mr Benn changes into his normal clothes and thanks the shopkeeper. "I liked that King" says Mr Benn "I'm glad he wasn't changed." "Thanks to you, Sir," says the shopkeeper.

Mr Benn walks home to 52, Festive Road. Nothing has changed here in this cheerful, ordinary street.

Good thinking, Mr Benn

The King is a good King: he rules his kingdom well and his people are happy. Yet the Queen is dissatisfied and so the people join with her in wanting the King to be different. But when Mr Benn casts his final spell and returns the King to normal everyone is overjoyed. This surprises Mr Benn as it is just how things were when he arrived.

Don't go looking for worries

The Queen orders a wizard to the Palace because a wizard can change things precisely, and make exactly what she wants to happen, happen. Little does she realise the consequences.

Be careful what you wish for, because it may just come true

Mr Benn finally puts his foot down and announces he will not keep changing the King to meet the Queen's capricious demands. He could continue casting spell upon spell but he refuses to, not thinking it right to continue.

Take the responsibility that
your position gives you

When the two men arrive in the wizard's cave and ask Mr Benn to come with them to the Palace he has only just picked up the book of useful spells. He is concerned he has not had time to cast a single practice spell. So before they leave the cavern he looks inside the book and reads that to do magic spells a wizard needs chalk, magic dust and a magic wand. He finds these three things and is ready.

Work out the minimum preparation

Mr Benn returns to Festive Road happy. He has restored good humour in a good kingdom by keeping things as they are, and he finds that Festive Road is just the same as when he left – ordinary. Just how he likes it.

Take as much delight in the ordinary
and the familiar as in the special

Zookeeper

SEEING THROUGH OTHERS' EYES

Where Mr Benn shows that you must treat others
as you would like to be treated

The story so far

Festive Road is unusually quiet today. Everybody seems to be indoors – even Mr Benn is sitting in his room, thinking how trapped he feels inside it today. So he decides to go to the costume shop. Just the walk along the streets does him good – he is glad to be out of his little room.

In the shop he is not sure which costume to choose; the shopkeeper suggests a dark blue uniform with a peaked cap. Who can it be, Mr Benn wonders. He tries on the costume and steps outside.

All around him there are tropical trees and the sounds of animals. Then he notices there are cages, with animals inside them – it's a zoo, and he must be the zookeeper.

But something is amiss in this zoo, the animals all look extremely miserable.

Soon Mr Benn finds himself in conversation with a parrot who explains what is wrong: the problem is purely that the cages are too small. Mr Benn ponders, and then has a plan.

The parrot loves the idea as do the animals when the parrot explains it to them. So, first things first, Mr Benn lets all the animals out of their cages and they hide amongst the trees and bushes.

Next, Mr Benn runs into the streets of the town calling out that all the animals have escaped from the zoo! A fearful crowd gathers and Mr Benn explains that as all the animals have left the zoo, that must now be the safest place for the people to be. In a frenzy of fright the crowd rushes to the zoo and the people squeeze and cram themselves into the animals' cages.

And wait.

Slowly the animals emerge one by one from their hiding places.

Mr Benn explains to the crowd that they needn't worry, the animals don't mean to harm them, they just wanted to illustrate that the cages are too small. "We see that now" say the squashed townsfolk. Mr Benn lets them out and together they all set to making bigger, better cages for the animals.

Mr Benn looks around for the parrot; a man appears to lead him into the parrot house, and Mr Benn is back in the shop. The shopkeeper gives Mr Benn a bright red feather – a present from the parrot.

Back in Festive Road things look the same, except that a neighbour has bought a larger birdcage for their pet parrot, and another has let their dog out of the car. Mr Benn smiles.

Good thinking, Mr Benn

When Mr Benn arrives as the new zoo keeper he looks around to take the measure of the place: he can see that the animals are not happy, but he doesn't understand why.

"Ah, that's better" says the parrot when Mr Benn lets him out of his cage.

Mr Benn knows how the parrot feels – he had felt trapped inside his little room – and now he understands. So he puts the people inside the cages – that will make them understand much better than explaining the problem would.

Showing is better than telling

Mr Benn is delighted to help make new cages for the animals, and he and the townspeople build them with alacrity. But the cages are not just bigger, they are also better – with slides and swings for play. The animals don't just need food and space, they need intellectual nourishment too.

Stimulate the mind

The animals are made miserable by the small cages, but otherwise, says the parrot, they like the zoo: in particular they like people looking at them perfectly well. With larger cages to spend their days in, the animals will be content to be the attention of people's gaze.

We need the right conditions
to entertain happily

Mr Benn trusts the parrot and animals won't escape when he lets them out of their cages. They trust him when he explains his plan: if they had not, nothing could have been changed in the zoo. (Of course, the people also trust Mr Benn, and that is their undoing! But it is all in a good cause.)

Trust others

Gladiator

BLOOD SPORTS

Where Mr Benn returns to Roman times
to show that cruelty will always catch up
with its perpetrators

Festive Road is very noisy today: workmen are everywhere, repairing the road. Mr Benn decides to take a walk to the costume shop. When he finds a Roman Gladiator's outfit he chuckles to himself, "The Romans made very good roads" he explains to the shopkeeper. The shopkeeper smiles and invites Mr Benn to try out the costume.

Mr Benn steps into the changing room and puts on the outfit of the Gladiator, helmet and all. Then he steps into another world.

He finds himself in open countryside surrounded by busy people; he recognises one of them – Smasher Lagru! What are they all doing? he asks Smasher. Building a road straight to the Arena in the city, Smasher tells Mr Benn. Just then a fanfare rings out and the Emperor arrives. Smasher gives Mr Benn a wink as he motions to a man holding a balancing instrument. The man places the equipment in the middle of the road, Smasher makes a short screech on a whistle …

… and the Emperor gives the thumbs up. "Lining up the road" explains Smasher. "The Emperor likes it and it gives us a break."

Indeed the Emperor likes it so much he tells Mr Benn that Smasher amuses him and to bring him to the Arena. But on the way Smasher explains why: prisoners are made to fight Gladiators in the Arena, and those who aren't beaten face the lions on the Emperor's signal. Mr Benn is not pleased – fighting is so silly. Smasher couldn't agree more.

Mr Benn is put in charge of the prisoners at the Arena and sees how miserable they are at the prospect of facing Gladiators then lions. Likewise the Gladiators are no more keen on the prospect of fighting. Then Smasher shows him where the lions are kept. Mr Benn has an idea.

Instead of fighting each other, the Gladiators and prisoners will play ball-games and tag in the Arena. But each time the Emperor is about to do thumbs down, signalling that someone should get a  squidging, Mr Benn blows Smasher's whistle and the man who sights the road looks to the Emperor from the roof of the Arena, and of course the Emperor has to give him the thumbs up.

The plan works brilliantly, and the crowd enjoy the games just as much as they did the fighting. But the Emperor is getting extremely annoyed that everyone is getting off squidge-free.

"Release the lions" he proclaims. Mr Benn does just that, but unfortunately for the Emperor he has changed the direction of the tunnel the lions run through to enter the Arena, and now it leads straight to the Emperor's seat.

The crowd don't stay to watch this rather different fight, and prisoners and Gladiators walk free.

Mr Benn and Smasher congratulate each other. "I'd better get back to that road" says Smasher. "See you again, Mr Benn." Mr Benn says he hopes so, just as a man appears and leads him away.

Mr Benn finds himself back in the shop. "Keep the whistle as a souvenir, Sir," says the shopkeeper. Mr Benn thanks him and waves goodbye. "See you soon" he says.

Good thinking, Mr Benn

Mr Benn chooses the Gladiator's costume because he is thinking of the Romans. He forgets that Gladiators are fighters, but later he very much finds out that they are.

Symbols have significance

The Emperor considered it sport to watch a prisoner die because he considered convicts worthless. Perhaps if he had come to know a prisoner, just as Mr Benn knew Smasher, he would have thought differently.

Familiarity reduces prejudice

Mr Benn saw that the Emperor enjoyed signalling the balance of the road, so in the Arena he told him that the road was in the Emperor's honour but they would need his help during the games to line it up. The Emperor nodded – of course they needed his help in completing it.

Self-important people
are so susceptible to flattery

The shopkeeper

As if by magic … the shopkeeper appeared. Of course the shopkeeper is magical. He sends Mr Benn on adventures in different worlds then he leads him back home. His costume shop doesn't just offer a variety of different outfits, it is alive with a million possibilities.

His cheery wave and smiling greeting make his exotic magical shop a homely place to be, but his purple Fez and uncanny knack of knowing which costume would best suit Mr Benn's day show that he is not an ordinary man. And his shop is not an ordinary business – Mr Benn never hires any of the costumes, he tries them out. The shopkeeper always invites him to return another day, for another adventure. Just as Mr Benn's subconscious would.

The shopkeeper doesn't guide Mr Benn in adventures – he always lets him discover the puzzle to be solved by himself, just as Mr Benn lets people see the solutions for themselves. The shopkeeper holds out a suggested costume to Mr Benn and simply points him in the direction of the changing room. The rest is up to him.

When Mr Benn has solved the problem and the wrong is righted, the shopkeeper appears. As if by magic. He leads Mr Benn back into the shop, back into his own world, just as the celebration is getting under way. He knows that in life it is always best to leave still wanting more. So as the people of the adventure-world anticipate the revelry ahead, Mr Benn steps back into his own life and into his own open future.

Open your mind to a world of possibilities